SPEAK
TO YOUR PET

My Guide To
Dog Training

Ashley Lee

Explore other books at:
WWW.ENGAGEBOOKS.COM

VANCOUVER, B.C.

WWW.ENGAGEBOOKS.COM

My Guide to Dog Training: Level 2
Speak to Your Pet
Lee, Ashley 1995 –
Text © 2022 Engage Books
Design © 2022 Engage Books

Edited by: A.R. Roumanis
Design by: A.R. Roumanis

Text set in Arial Regular.
Chapter headings set in Arial Black.

FIRST EDITION / FIRST PRINTING

LIBRARY AND ARCHIVES CANADA CATALOGUING IN PUBLICATION

Title: My guide to dog training / Ashley Lee.
Other titles: Dog training
Names: Lee, Ashley, 1995- author.

Description: Series statement: Speak to your pet |
Engaging readers: level 2, reading with help.

Identifiers: Canadiana (print) 20210394234 | Canadiana (ebook) 20210394358
ISBN 978-1-77476-659-0 (hardcover)
ISBN 978-1-77476-660-6 (softcover)
ISBN 978-1-77476-662-0 (pdf)
ISBN 978-1-77476-661-3 (epub)

Subjects:
LCSH: Readers (Elementary).
LCSH: Readers—Dogs—Training.
LCSH: Readers (Publications).

Classification: LCC PE1119.2 .L445 2022 | DDC J428.6/2—DC23

This project has been made possible in part by the Government of Canada.

Canada

Contents

Why Should I Train My Dog?

A dog that is well behaved and can follow the rules has a better chance at staying safe. If a dog can "come" or "stay," they are less likely to run into the road or get lost.

Training your dog can help you bond with them. You and your dog will love and trust each other even more.

SAFETY TIP:

Always have an adult supervise your training sessions to make sure you and your dog are staying safe.

What Is My Dog Trying to Tell Me?

A happy dog will have their ears up and mouth open. They may also stick their tongue out.

An angry dog will wrinkle their nose and show their teeth. They may also pull their ears back.

A scared dog will pull their ears back and may stick their neck out.

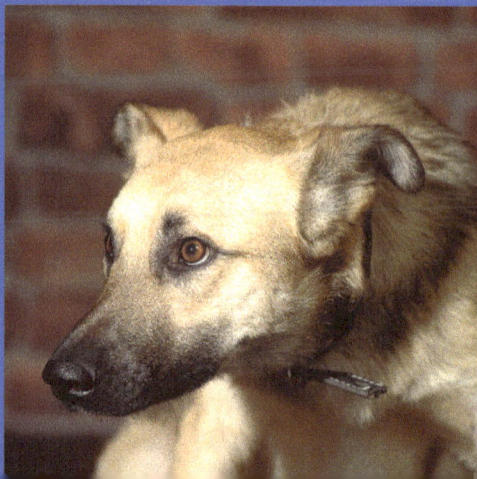

A happy dog will keep their tail down and may swing it from side to side.

An angry dog will keep their tail close to their body. The hair on their back may stand up.

A scared dog will tuck their tail between their legs and lower their head.

What Is the Best Way to Train My Dog?

The best place to train is in a quiet area with few distractions. Train for about fifteen minutes every day, either all at once or five minutes at a time. It can be helpful to start with shorter training sessions.

Every dog has different needs. Some dogs take longer to learn than others. If you or your dog get irritated, stop training and try again another day.

SAFETY TIP:
Never yell at your dog or hit them. This can cause them to bite you.

9

What Tools Do I Need to Train My Dog?

Healthy treats: Using small treats will help make sure your dog doesn't get too full.

Clicker: A clicker is a small device with a button that makes a clicking sound when you press it.

Toys: If treats don't make your dog excited, use toys instead.

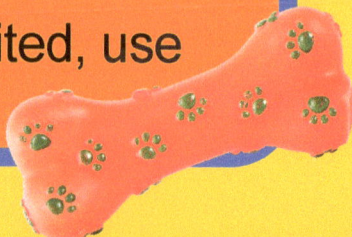

Leash and harness: If you plan on training outside, make sure to use a leash and harness so your dog doesn't run off.

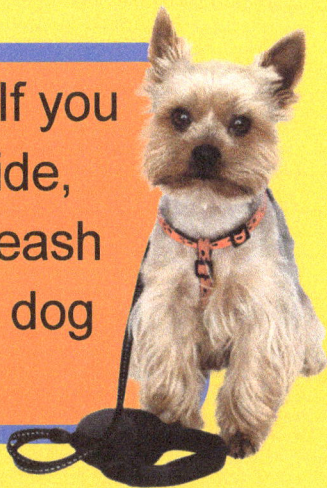

Water: Training is hard work! Make sure your dog drinks plenty of water.

Beginner Lesson 1: Charging Your Clicker

Charging your clicker means getting your dog used to it so they know the click sound means they get a treat. Here is how to charge your clicker.

1 Click the clicker and give your dog a treat at the same time. Repeat four or five times.

2 Next, click the clicker first, then toss the treat in front of your dog so they have to move to get it. Repeat four or five times.

3 Repeat steps 1 and 2 for several days in a row. If your dog looks at you for a treat when they hear the clicker, you're ready to move on. If not, repeat the steps for a few more days.

Beginner Lesson 2: Come

1 Sit close to your dog with your hand held towards them and say "come." Click and give them a treat if they come to you. If they don't come, move closer and try again. Repeat four or five times.

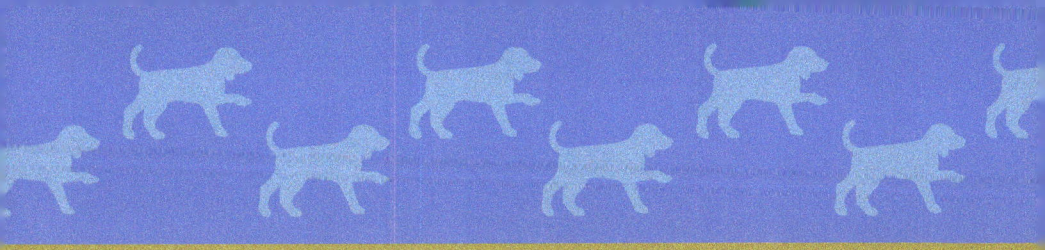

2 Move a few steps back and repeat step 1 four or five times.

3 Repeat every day. Move farther away from your dog as they improve.

Beginner Lesson 3: Sit

1   Hold a treat in front of your dog's nose.
    Slowly move your hand up as your dog
    follows the treat with their eyes

2   As your dog tilts their head up,
    their back end will lower until they
    are in a sitting position.

3 Click the clicker and say "sit" while giving your dog a treat. Repeat four or five times a day for several days.

4 Click the clicker and tell your dog to "sit." Don't hold a treat in front of your dog. If they sit, give them a treat. If they don't, repeat steps 1 through 3 for a few more days.

Beginner Lesson 4: Stay

1 Have your dog sit in front of you. Say "stay" while holding your hand out in front of you. Stay here for no more than two seconds.

2 Drop your hand and say "okay," then give your dog a treat. Saying "okay" lets them know it is okay to move now.

3 Repeat steps 1 and 2 for several days, slowly increasing the amount of time your dog stays before getting the treat.

4 Once your dog can stay for 30 seconds, have your dog sit and stay while you take a step back and repeat step 2. Slowly increase the distance between you and your dog as they learn to stay.

Advanced Lesson 1: Shake a Paw

1 Have your dog sit in front of you. Gently pick up one paw. At the same time, click the clicker and say "shake."

2 Give your dog a treat then gently lower its paw.

3 Repeat four or five times a day for several days. To help your dog learn the trick faster, use the same paw each time.

4 Put your hand out and say "shake" without clicking the clicker. Give your dog a treat if they offer you their paw. Repeat steps 1 through 3 if they don't.

Advanced Lesson 2: Spin

1 Hold a treat in front of your dog's nose. Slowly make a large circle around your dog's body.

2 If they follow your hand and make a full circle, click and give them the treat. If not, try again.

3 Repeat 4 or 5 times a day for several days.

4 Once your dog is comfortable with this, say "spin" as you move your hand in a circle. Repeat until they can perform the trick when only hearing the word "spin."

Advanced Lesson 3: Down

1 Have your dog sit. Hold a treat in front of their nose and lower it to the ground. Your dog should follow the treat with their nose.

2 Move the treat along the ground away from your dog. Your dog should continue to follow the treat with their nose.

3 When your dog is in the down position, click the clicker and give them the treat. Repeat four or five times a day for several days.

4 Repeat steps 1 through 3 while holding the treat in your other hand and saying "down." Click the clicker and give them a treat when they complete the trick.

Advanced Lesson 4: Quiet

1 Wait for your dog to bark.

2 Say "quiet" and wait for your dog to stop barking.

3 When your dog stops barking, click the clicker and give them a treat.

4 Repeat each time your dog barks. Keep in mind that this trick can take weeks or even months to learn.

Super Training

Time and patience is all it takes to teach your dog some amazing tricks. Do you think you could teach your dog to do any of these tricks?

Surf's up! Many dogs can be taught to ride through the waves on a surfboard. How cool is that?

Fetch is great, but what about soccer? Some dogs will naturally kick a ball around, while others need a bit more training.

Dog dancing is a combination of a bunch of different tricks. The results are so fun to watch!

Quiz

Test your knowledge of dog training by answering the following questions. The questions are based on what you have read in this book. The answers are listed on the bottom of the next page.

1 What does it mean if a dog's nose is wrinkled?

2 What does it mean if a dog swings its tail from side to side?

3 Where is the best place to train?

4 How long should you spend training your dog each day?

5 What should you do if you or your dog are getting irritated during a training session?

6 Why should you use small treats when training your dog?

Explore Other Level 2 Readers.

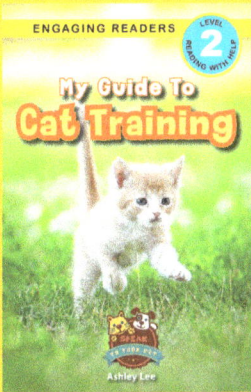

ENGAGING READERS — LEVEL 2 — READING WITH HELP
My Guide To Cat Training
Ashley Lee

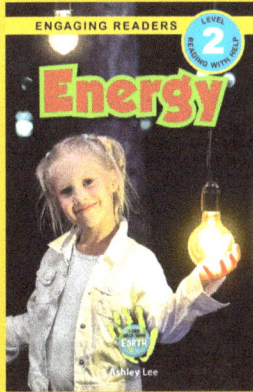

ENGAGING READERS — LEVEL 2 — READING WITH HELP
Energy
Ashley Lee

ENGAGING READERS — LEVEL 2 — READING WITH HELP
Food
Ashley Lee

ENGAGING READERS — LEVEL 2 — READING WITH HELP
Plastics
Ashley Lee

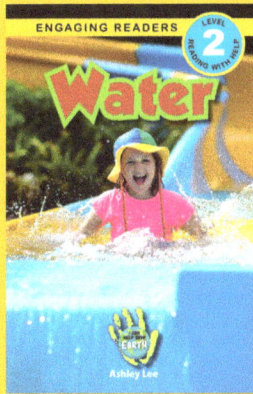

ENGAGING READERS — LEVEL 2 — READING WITH HELP
Water
Ashley Lee

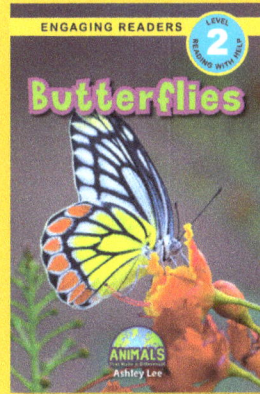

ENGAGING READERS — LEVEL 2 — READING WITH HELP
Butterflies
Ashley Lee

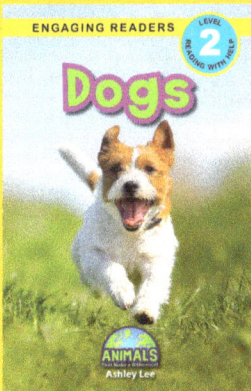

ENGAGING READERS — LEVEL 2 — READING WITH HELP
Dogs
Ashley Lee

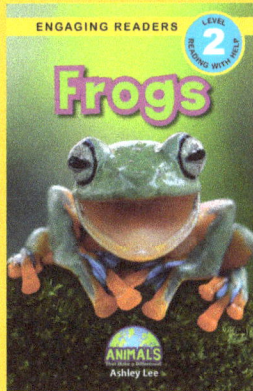

ENGAGING READERS — LEVEL 2 — READING WITH HELP
Frogs
Ashley Lee

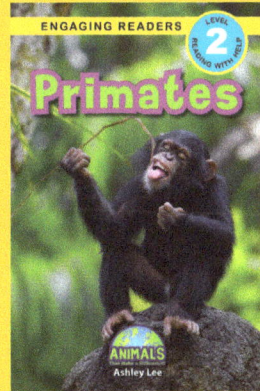

ENGAGING READERS — LEVEL 2 — READING WITH HELP
Primates
Ashley Lee

Visit www.engagebooks.com/readers

Answers:
1. It is angry 2. It is happy 3. In a quiet area with few distraction 4. About 15 minutes 5. Stop and try again another day 6. So they don't get too full

31

www.ingramcontent.com/pod-product-compliance
Lightning Source LLC
Chambersburg PA
CBHW051238020426
42331CB00016B/3435